Good Question!

How Does a Caterpillar Become a Butterfly?
AND OTHER QUESTIONS ABOUT . . .
Butterflies

STERLING CHILDREN'S BOOKS
New York

STERLING CHILDREN'S BOOKS
New York

An Imprint of Sterling Publishing
387 Park Avenue South
New York, NY 10016

Text © 2014 Melissa Stewart
Illustrations © 2014 Sterling Publishing Co., Inc.
Photo credits: Corbis © Michael & Patricia Fogden: 26; © Caisii Mao/Demotix: 17; © Joe McDonald: 8; iStockphoto © gornostaj: 20;
© SF photo: 9; Shutterstock © Olga Bogatryenko: 17 inset; © Nikola Rahme: 24; © StevenRussellSmithPhotos: 25; © Luna Vandoorne: 21

ISBN 978-1-4549-0666-7 (hardcover)
ISBN 978-1-4549-0667-4 (paperback)

Library of Congress Cataloging-in-Publication Data

Stewart, Melissa.
  How does a caterpillar become a butterfly? : and other questions about butterflies / by Melissa Stewart ; illustrated by Annie Patterson.
    pages cm. -- (Good question!)
  Includes bibliographical references and index.
   ISBN 978-1-4549-0667-4 (pbk.) -- ISBN 978-1-4549-0666-7 (hardcover) 1. Butterflies--Life cycles--Juvenile literature. I. Title.
QL544.2.S7455 2014
595.78'9156--dc23
                                                                                          2013022927

Distributed in Canada by Sterling Publishing
c/o Canadian Manda Group, 165 Dufferin Street
Toronto, Ontario, Canada M6K 3H6
Distributed in the United Kingdom by GMC Distribution Services
Castle Place, 166 High Street, Lewes, East Sussex, England BN7 1XU
Distributed in Australia by Capricorn Link (Australia) Pty. Ltd.
P.O. Box 704, Windsor, NSW 2756, Australia

Design by Jennifer Browning and Elizabeth Phillips
Art by Annie Patterson

For information about custom editions, special sales, and premium and corporate purchases, please contact Sterling Special Sales at 800-805-5489 or
specialsales@sterlingpublishing.com.

Manufactured in China
Lot #:
2 4 6 8 10 9 7 5 3 1
10/13

www.sterlingpublishing.com/kids

CONTENTS

What is a butterfly? 5

What is a caterpillar?..6

How did the caterpillar get its name? 6

Why do some caterpillars have spiky hairs on their bodies? 9

How else do caterpillars protect themselves? 9

What do caterpillars do all day?.................................10

What happens when a caterpillar gets too big for its skin?...................10

How does a caterpillar become a butterfly?.............12

From Caterpillar to Pupa 13

From Pupa to Adult 14

How does a butterfly escape from its chrysalis? 15

What is metamorphosis? 15

What do butterflies eat? 16

How do butterflies help plants? 16

Can butterflies taste with their feet? 19

How does a butterfly see, smell, and feel?.................19

How do butterflies protect themselves from enemies? 20

Monarch Migration Routes 22

What do butterflies do when the weather turns cold?.................................23

How is a butterfly different from a moth? 24

How do butterflies make more butterflies?...................26

Do butterflies need our help? 28

A Butterfly's Life Cycle 30

Find Out More..31

Index 32

The Queen Alexandra's birdwing lives in the tropical rain forests of Southeast Asia.

What is a butterfly?

A butterfly is an insect. So are bees and beetles, ants and grasshoppers.

An insect's body has three main parts. The head is in the front. The thorax is in the middle. The abdomen is the part at the back. An insect's body is covered with a hard exoskeleton that protects its soft insides.

An insect has six legs attached to its thorax. A butterfly can rest on its legs, but it can't walk very well. Many insects also have wings. An adult butterfly has two sets of big, beautiful wings.

More than 18,000 kinds of butterflies live on Earth today, and about 750 kinds live in North America. They make their homes in fields, forests, gardens, and wetlands. A few kinds of butterflies can live in hot, dry deserts.

Butterflies come in many sizes and colors. The Queen Alexandra's birdwing is the world's largest butterfly. Its wings stretch wider than the pages in this book. But the tiny pygmy blue butterfly is about the size of your thumbnail.

This pygmy blue butterfly is shown at actual size.

What is a caterpillar?

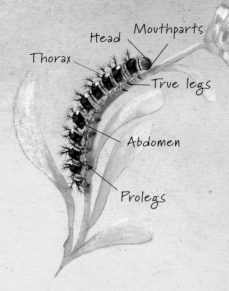

Some young insects look like tiny adults. They are called nymphs. But many young insects don't look anything like their parents. They are called larvae. The larvae of flies are called maggots. The larvae of bees and beetles are called grubs. The larvae of butterflies and moths are called caterpillars.

Like all insects, a caterpillar has three main body parts that are protected by a hard exoskeleton. A caterpillar doesn't have wings, but it does have six legs attached to its thorax. And that's not all! It also has ten stubby prolegs attached to its abdomen. Prolegs help a caterpillar crawl from place to place. Suction pads on the ends of the prolegs can hold on tight to leaves and stems.

How else are caterpillars different from their parents? Adult butterflies have two large eyes, and they use the long, thin antennae on their heads to sense the world. Caterpillars don't have antennae, but they can have as many as twelve eyes.

How did the caterpillar get its name?

Long ago, people didn't know that a caterpillar is a young butterfly or moth. They thought caterpillars were more like worms than insects, so they came up with different names for the young and the adult.

The word *caterpillar* comes from Old French. It means "hairy cat." Why did the larva get such a strange name? People thought it looked like a tiny cat with long, spiky hairs.

This American painted lady caterpillar is munching on burdock leaves.

When the spicebush swallowtail bends its head under its body, eyespots on its thorax fool predators. They make the caterpillar look like a snake.

Why do some caterpillars have spiky hairs on their bodies?

A red admiral caterpillar has sharp, spiny hairs all over its body. So does a common buckeye caterpillar. The spiky hairs, or spines, help these caterpillars stay safe. They make the larvae look bigger and scarier than they really are, so some predators leave them alone. Other enemies back off for an even better reason: They don't want to end up with a mouthful of sharp spikes.

A saddleback caterpillar's spines are just as scary as they look. When an enemy attacks, the spikes cut into its skin. Poison flows through the spines and into the attacker's body. The painful sting makes the predator feel sick.

How else do caterpillars protect themselves?

Caterpillars have lots of enemies. Birds, toads, mice, rats, and skunks all hunt caterpillars. So do some other insects. It's a good thing caterpillars have lots of different tricks for staying safe.

The common wood nymph caterpillar is all green, so it has no trouble blending in with its surroundings. A viceroy caterpillar looks like bird poop, so predators stay away. A spicebush swallowtail has two eyespots that make it look like a snake. The bright colors of a monarch caterpillar send out a warning that says, "Don't eat me. I taste bad."

Common buckeye caterpillar

What do caterpillars do all day?

Caterpillars munch and crunch and chomp and chew. They eat all day long. Some caterpillars eat at night, too.

Like all insects, a caterpillar begins life inside an egg. When it's ready to enter the world, the larva chews a hole in the hard, waxy shell and wriggles out.

A caterpillar's first meal is usually its eggshell, which is full of nutrients. Then the little larva gorges on leaves, buds, flowers, and stems. It eats and grows, eats and grows.

What happens when a caterpillar gets too big for its skin?

As a caterpillar grows, its soft insides press against its hard outside. But the exoskeleton doesn't budge. It can't. As the hard outer skin gets tighter and tighter, the larva has trouble getting enough air to breathe. Finally, the young insect knows it's time to shed its exoskeleton. This process is called molting.

The caterpillar stops eating. It twists and turns, wriggles and squirms. Rip! A jagged crack races down the larva's back. Then the caterpillar heaves its body out of the split skin.

At first, the new exoskeleton is soft. The caterpillar fills its body with air to stretch the flexible skin and make more room for growing. Then it takes a short break and goes back to eating.

Zebra longwing caterpillars spend most of their time feeding on passion fruit leaves.

How does a caterpillar become a butterfly?

After leaving its egg, a caterpillar eats and grows for one or two weeks. During that period it molts four or five times. Just before the final molt, the larva searches for a safe spot. Some caterpillars crawl to the ground and hide under leaves. Others, like the monarch caterpillar, spin out a bit of sticky silk and attach themselves to a twig or strong leaf stem.

As soon as a larva sheds its skin for the last time, we call it a pupa. Its body is surrounded by a hard, protective wrapper called a chrysalis. It takes a monarch caterpillar twelve to fifteen hours to create its chrsalis. A chrysalis stays still, but lots of changes are happening inside. The pupa's whole body breaks down, and then the insect rebuilds all its parts. Its new head is smaller, and it has antennae. A coiled sipping straw replaces its jaws. Its legs stretch longer, and it grows wings. It's an amazing process.

Some pupae take just a few days to go through all the changes, but others need a few weeks, months, or even years to become butterflies.

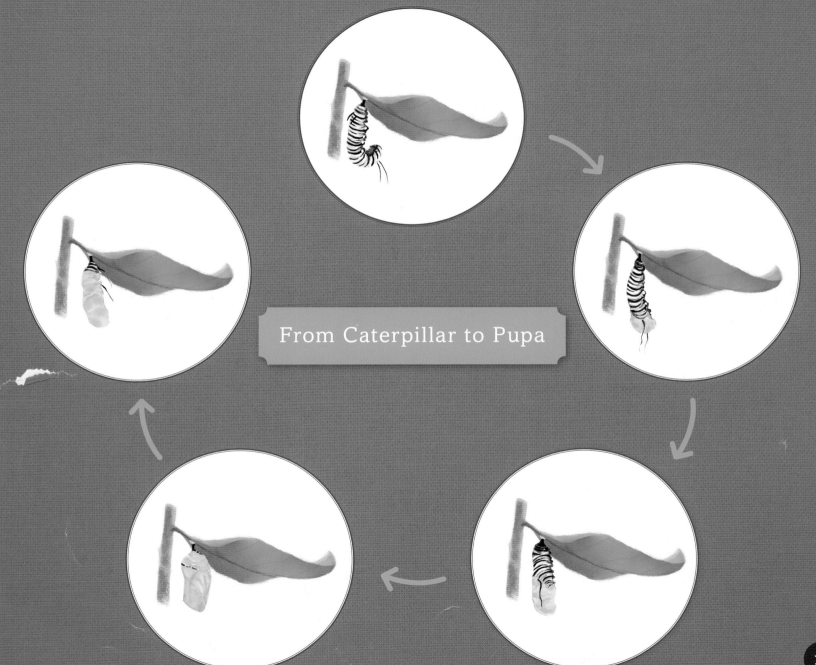

From Caterpillar to Pupa

13

From Pupa to Adult

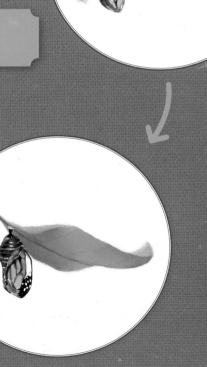

How does a butterfly escape from its chrysalis?

Just as a monarch pupa finishes changing into an adult, its green chrysalis loses its color. That makes it easy to see the cramped, crumpled insect inside. The trapped butterfly is ready to make its escape.

The butterfly pushes against the hard shell until it cracks. Then the chrysalis splits in half, and the butterfly pushes its legs and antennae through the opening. Its legs grasp the outside of the case and pull the rest of its body out.

At first, the butterfly is wet and sticky. Its wings seem tiny, but its abdomen is huge. As the butterfly's body dries, its wings slowly unfold. The insect pumps fluid out of its abdomen and into its wings. Now it can spread its wings wide and let them dry and harden.

After about thirty minutes, the butterfly is ready for its first flight. It flaps its wings and soars off into the sky.

What is metamorphosis?

Metamorphosis comes from a Greek word that means "to change in shape or form." Insects go through metamorphosis. So do frogs. These animals go through lots of changes as they grow up. In butterflies, metamorphosis has four stages: egg, larva, pupa, and adult.

What do butterflies eat?

A caterpillar has strong jaws that are perfect for grinding leaves and stems. But an adult butterfly feeds with a long, thin tube called a proboscis.

Most of the time, a butterfly's proboscis stays curled up tight. At mealtime, the long tongue rolls out and slurps up food. It works like a drinking straw.

Most butterflies sip nectar, a sweet liquid that flowers make. Butterflies with long proboscises can reach deep inside flowers, while butterflies with short proboscises have to feed on flowers with easy-to-reach nectar.

Some butterflies would rather dine on tree sap or juices from rotting fruit. A few butterflies suck up juices from dead animals or rotting poop.

Some butterflies like a little bit of salt in their diets. Besides feeding on nectar or other sugary juices, they also sip salts from muddy puddles.

How do butterflies help plants?

As a butterfly sips sweet juices from a flower, tiny bits of powdery flower pollen stick to its body. When the insect flies to another flower, the pollen goes along for the ride.

If some of the pollen falls off the butterfly and lands on another flower, a tiny tube opens up inside the flower. When the pollen reaches the bottom of the tube, some of the material inside the pollen mixes with material from the flower. If the conditions are just right, new seeds will form, and some of those seeds will grow into new plants. Many kinds of plants couldn't survive without butterflies and bees to spread their pollen.

This butterfly is using its long proboscis to sip nectar from a bright pink flower.

This butterfly has a curled up proboscis.

As this orange tip butterfly flits through the air, its eyes and antennae help it understand its surroundings.

Can butterflies taste with their feet?

You bet! Taste sensors on their feet tell them what kind of plant they have landed on. Most butterflies drink nectar from many kinds of flowers, but caterpillars are picky eaters. Many of them eat just one kind of plant. For example, monarch caterpillars only eat milkweed, and karner blues only eat wild blue lupine. That means female butterflies have to be sure to lay their eggs on the right kind of plant. The taste sensors on their feet let them know when they have found it.

How does a butterfly see, smell, and feel?

Butterflies have two eyes, just like you, but they don't see the world in the same way. The lens inside each of your eyes gives you a complete view of your surroundings, but a butterfly has compound eyes with thousands of little lenses. Because each lens gets a slightly different view of the world, a butterfly can see right and left, up and down all at the same time. It can also detect even the tiniest movements.

In between a butterfly's eyes are two long, thin antennae that help the insect smell and feel. Butterflies depend on their antennae to find food and sense how the wind is blowing.

How do butterflies protect themselves from enemies?

Butterflies escape from hungry ants, toads, rats, lizards, and snakes by taking flight. But flying can't keep butterflies safe all the time. They still have to be on the lookout for birds and dragonflies. Luckily, butterflies can use some of the same tricks as caterpillars.

Monarch butterflies taste awful, so most predators spit them out. The butterfly's bright colors help hunters remember not to make the same mistake twice. Zebra butterflies don't taste bad, but they sure do stink. When they perch in large groups, no predator dares to come near.

A brimstone butterfly's green wings are shaped like a leaf, and that makes it hard to spot when it rests on a tree. A comma butterfly can hide on the forest floor because its wings look like dead leaves.

The bottoms of a blue morpho butterfly's wings match its surroundings, too. But it also has another trick. When an enemy gets too close, the butterfly flashes the bright blue colors on the tops of its wings. That startles the predator just long enough for the morpho to escape.

Wood nymphs and pearly-eyes have spots on their wings that look like eyes. They fool birds into grabbing the butterflies' wings instead of biting off their heads.

The underside of the blue morpho's wings are brown to blend in with its surroundings.

The blue morpho flashes its bright blue wings to startle enemies.

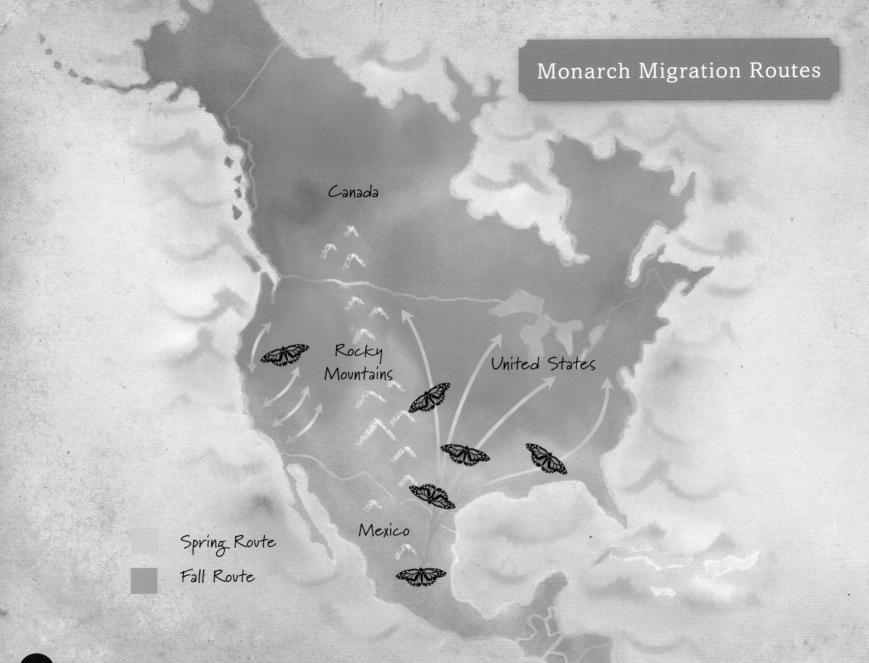

Monarch Migration Routes

Canada

Rocky
Mountains

United States

Mexico

Spring Route

Fall Route

What do butterflies do when the weather turns cold?

Some butterflies migrate, or fly to warmer parts of the world, when the weather turns cold. Monarch butterflies that live in the eastern half of North America fly to a mountaintop forest in Mexico. All winter long, they rest together in tall trees. Monarchs that live in the western half of North America fly to the coast of California.

Monarchs aren't the only kind of butterflies that migrate. The passion butterfly heads to Florida. Common buckeyes and cloudless sulphurs fly to sites all over Mexico.

But not all butterflies migrate. Mourning cloaks find safe, cozy spots in the woods and rest, or hibernate, through the winter. Comma butterflies and question mark butterflies hibernate in woodpiles or under loose tree bark.

Bronze copper larvae pass the winter inside their eggs. Scientists think that half of all butterflies spend the winter as caterpillars. Some caterpillars stay warm by burrowing underground. Viceroys and red spotted purple caterpillars hide inside rolled up leaves.

Gray hairstreaks and some swallowtails pass the winter as pupae. Their chrysalises protect them from the cold. At the first sign of spring, these insects break free and make their first flight.

How is a butterfly different from a moth?

Moths and butterflies might look similar, but they belong to two different groups of insects. Here are four easy ways to tell them apart.

1. A butterfly's antennae are long and thin with a knob on the end. A moth's antennae are short and feathery.
2. Most butterflies fly during the day and rest at night. Most moths fly at night and rest during the day.
3. A butterfly has a thin, smooth coat of scales on its wings. A moth's wing scales form a thick, fuzzy coat that helps the insect stay warm on cool nights.
4. A butterfly rests with its wings closed. On cool mornings, it spreads its wings wide to soak up sunlight. A moth always rests with its wings open.

This photograph shows a magnified view of a moth's wing scales.

   Have you heard that all butterflies have bright, colorful wings? Or that all moths have brown or gray wings? Don't believe it. The next time you see a large-winged insect flitting through the air, don't look at its color. Think about the time of day. Look at the insect's antennae and scales, and watch how it perches. Then you'll know if it's a butterfly or a moth.

A luna moth has short, feathery antennae and rests with its wings spread wide.

How do butterflies make more butterflies?

During certain times of the year, a female's abdomen is packed full of eggs. But she can't lay them until she finds a mate.

How does she attract a male? She makes a strong-smelling scent that fills the air and travels on the wind. She also uses her antennae to pick up scent messages sent out by males. The messages say, "Here I am. Come find me."

When a male and female find one another, they turn back to back, raise their wings high, and press their abdomens together. After the male's sperm mixes with his mate's eggs, the female can lay her eggs.

But she must choose a spot carefully, knowing that her youngsters will be picky eaters. Each time she lands on a leaf, she tastes it with her feet to see if it is the right kind of plant.

Most females lay more than one hundred eggs. But many of them are eaten by predators. Rain and wind destroy some, too. Only a few of the eggs a female lays will develop into caterpillars.

But that's enough. Butterflies have lived on Earth for more than 200 million years. They were alive when dinosaurs roamed the earth, and they are still with us today.

Clearwing butterflies mating

This pierid butterfly lives in the tropical rain forests of Central and South America. She will lay between twenty and eighty eggs.

Do butterflies need our help?

Many kinds of butterflies are having trouble surviving. In some places, butterflies have no place to live because workers have cut down forests and bulldozed wetlands to build houses, schools, and businesses. In other places, butterflies lost their homes when farmers plowed grassy fields to plant crops.

Some butterflies die when people spray poisons to kill mosquitoes. Others have nowhere to go when climate change—caused by burning oil to heat homes and using gasoline to power cars—heats up the insects' mountaintop homes.

In the United States, the U.S. Fish and Wildlife Service keeps track of creatures that are in danger of going extinct. Right now, there are more than twenty kinds of butterflies on the U.S. Endangered Species List. Scientists are studying another dozen butterflies to see if they should be added.

The good news is that lots of people are working to save butterflies. And you can help. Here are some ideas:

>> Don't catch and keep butterflies.

>> Join a group of people tracking butterflies in your area.

>> Don't spray chemicals that might harm butterflies.

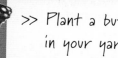

>> Plant a butterfly garden in your yard or at school.

>> Ask your friends and family to help.

This butterfly garden includes butterfly bushes, foxglove, salvia, and other plants with delicious nectar.

A Butterfly's Life Cycle

Larva (caterpillar)

Pupa (chrysalis)

Egg

Adult (butterfly)

FIND OUT MORE

Books to Read

Aston, Dianna Hutts. *A Butterfly Is Patient*. San Francisco, CA: Chronicle Books, 2011.

Bishop, Nic. *Butterflies and Moths.* New York: Scholastic, 2009.

Murawski, Darlyne. *Face to Face with Butterflies.* Washington, D.C.: National Geographic, 2010.

Schappert, Phil. *A World for Butterflies: Their Lives, Behavior and Future.* Richmond Hill, Ontario, Canada: Firefly Books, 2000.

Stewart, Melissa. *A Place for Butterflies*. Atlanta, GA: Peachtree, 2006.

Wright, Amy Bartlett. *Peterson First Guide to Caterpillars of North America.* Boston: Houghton Mifflin, 1998.

Websites to Visit

BUTTERFLIES OF NORTH AMERICA
www.butterfliesandmoths.org

BUTTERFLIES FOR KIDS
www.butterfliesforkids.org

THE BUTTERFLY WEBSITE
www.butterflywebsite.com

THE CHILDREN'S BUTTERFLY SITE
www.kidsbutterfly.org

For bibliography and free activities visit: http://www.sterlingpublishing.com/kids/good-question

INDEX

A

Abdomen, 5, 15, 26
Antennae, 6, 12, 18, 19, 24, 25, 26

B

Blue morpho butterfly, 20–21
Brimstone butterfly, 20
Bronze copper larvae, 23
Butterflies
  body parts, 5, 16
  caterpillars becoming, 12–13
  caterpillars compared to, 6
  in cold weather, 22–23
  eating, 16, 17, 19
  endangered, 28
  escaping from chrysalis, 14–15
  helping, 28
  helping plants, 16
  hibernating, 23
  kinds of, 5, 23
  largest and smallest, 5
  life cycle, illustrated, 30
  making more butterflies, 26
  metamorphosis of, 15
  migrating, 22, 23
  moths compared to, 24–25
  protection from enemies, 20–21
  seeing, smelling, and feeling, 19
  stages of development, 15
  tasting with feet, 19
  what they are, 5

C

Caterpillars
  becoming butterflies, 12–13
  butterflies compared to, 6

  in cold weather, 23
  daily routine, 10
  eating and growing, 10, 11, 12
  food for, 7
  "hairy cat" and, 6
  hibernating, 23
  molting (shedding) skin, 10, 12
  naming of, 6, 9
  as nymphs, 6
  protection from enemies, 9
  pupae and, 12–13, 23
  spiny hairs on, 9
  what they are, 6
Chrysalises, 12–15, 23
Cloudless sulphurs, 23
Comma butterflies, 20, 23
Common buckeye caterpillar, 9, 23

E

Eating. *See* Food, eating
Eggs, 10, 15, 17, 23, 26, 27
Endangered butterflies, 28
Enemies, protection from, 9, 20–21
Exoskeleton, 5, 6, 10
Eyes, 6, 18, 19
Eyespots, 8, 9, 20

F

Feeling. *See* Antennae
Feet, tasting with, 19
Food, eating
  butterflies, 16, 19
  caterpillars, 10, 11, 12

G

Gray hairstreaks, 23

H

Helping butterflies, 28
Hibernation, 23

I

Insects
  beginning life, 10
  body parts, 5
  as larvae, 6
  number of legs, 5

L

Legs, 5, 6, 12, 15
Life cycle, illustrated, 30

M

Mating, 26. *See also* Eggs
Metamorphosis, 15
Migration, of butterflies, 22, 23
Molting, 10, 12
Monarch butterflies, 15, 20, 22, 23
Monarch caterpillars and pupae, 9,
  12–15, 19
Moths, 24–25
Mourning cloaks, 23

N

Nectar, 16, 17, 19
Nymphs, 6

P

Plants, butterflies helping, 16
Pollen, 16
Proboscis, 16, 17
Prolegs, 6
Protecting butterflies, 28

Protection
  butterflies, 20–21
  caterpillars, 8–9
Pupae, 12–13, 23

Q

Queen Alexandra's birdwing, 4, 5
Question mark butterflies, 23

R

Red spotted purple caterpillars, 23
Reproduction, 26. *See also* Eggs

S

Saddleback caterpillar, 9
Seeing. *See* Eyes
Senses, of butterflies, 19
Skin, molting, 10, 12
Smelling. *See* Antennae
Spiny hairs, 9
Swallowtails, 23

T

Tasting, with feet, 19
Thorax, 5, 6, 8

V

Viceroys, 9, 23

W

Wings, 5, 12, 15, 20, 24
Winter, butterflies in, 22, 23
Wood nymphs, 9, 20

Z

Zebra butterflies, 11, 20